ScottFor
In Contact 1

PART B

CHARLES RAHT
Institute of North American Studies
Barcelona, Spain

BARBARA R. DENMAN
Prince George's County Adult Education Program
Prince George's County, Maryland

N. ELIZABETH LAVIE
The British Council

SANDRA J. BRIGGS
San Mateo Union High School District
San Mateo, California

SERIES CONSULTANTS

JAMES E. PURPURA
Institute of North American Studies
Barcelona, Spain

DIANE PINKLEY
Institute of North American Studies
Badalona, Spain

🔳 ScottForesman
A Division of HarperCollinsPublishers

I would like to thank my family, friends and colleagues who have helped me to complete this book. Similarly, thanks are due to the editorial staff of Scott, Foresman and Company from whom I received considerable guidance throughout the project. Most of all, I want to thank Kevin Rimmington who gave me advice, support, and encouragement throughout this seemingly endless endeavor: ta, Kev.

Charles Raht

I would like to thank Mark, Charles, Alex, and Teddy for their help and support during this project. I would also like to thank the staff at Scott, Foresman and Company: Tim Collins for getting me into this, and Judy Mendel and Chris Williams for getting me through it.

Barbara R. Denman

CONSULTING REVIEWERS

Anna Marie Amudi, *Dhahran Ahliyya Schools*
Dammam, Saudi Arabia

Augusto Baratau, *American Language School*
Guayaquil, Ecuador

Tracy Caldwell Gavilanes, *Pontificia Universidad Católica del Ecuador*
Quito, Ecuador

Antonio Cervellino, *Chilean Ministry of Education*
Santiago, Chile

Manuel C. R. Dos Santos, *ELT Author/Consultant*
Curitiba, Brazil

Barbara A. Encinas, *Mesa Community College*
Mesa, Arizona

Miriam García de Bermúdez, *Universidad de Costa Rica*
San Jose, Costa Rica

Stephen Gudgel, *Institute of North American Studies*
Barcelona, Spain

Mario Herrera Salazar, *Director, Language Center of the Normal Superior of Nuevo Leon*
Monterrey, Mexico

Carlos Alberto Hoffmann de Mendonça, *Colegio Pedro II*
Rio de Janeiro, Brazil

Titika Magaliou, *Athens College*
Athens, Greece

Juana I. Marín, *Catedrática, Escuela Oficial de Idiomas de Madrid*
Madrid, Spain

Ricardo F. Marzo, *Director, ELS-Peru*
Lima, Peru

Lourdes Montoró, M.A., Philologist, *Escola Tècnica Professional d'Hostafrancs*
Barcelona, Spain

Diane E. Özbal, *Robert College*
Istanbul, Turkey

Jose Javier Preciado Ceseña, *Universidad Nacional Autonoma de Mexico, Centro Universitario Mexico*
Mexico City, Mexico

Issam Safady, *University of Jordan, English Department*
Amman, Jordan

Christine Zaher, M.A., M. Ed., *The American University in Cairo*
Cairo, Egypt

Abla Zuraykat, *Ahliyyah School for Girls*
Amman, Jordan

We wish to thank the following people for their assistance in preparing these materials.

Maria Frias, *Colegio/Instituto Bachillerato Ramiro de Maeztu*
Madrid, Spain

Ramon Palencia, *Instituto Bachillerato Maria Zambrano*
Madrid, Spain

Colegio Viaro
Barcelona, Spain

Bonnie Baker, John Hang, *Institute of North American Studies*
Barcelona, Spain

Illustration and photography credits will be found on page 108.

ISBN: 0-673-19567-8

CONTENTS

WARM UP

What kind of exercise do you like to do? How often do you do it? Do you think you are in shape?

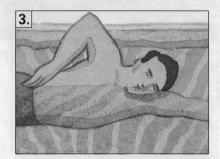

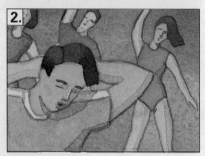

EXERCISE 1: *What Can You Do at a Health Club?*

Look at the pictures. Write the numbers.

a. _____ swim   **d.** _____ exercise   **g.** _____ ride exercise bikes
b. _____ run   **e.** _____ jump rope   **h.** _____ play basketball
c. _____ lift weights   **f.** _____ walk

EXERCISE 2: *Do You Like to Swim?*

Work with a partner. Look at Exercise 1. What does your partner like to do? Ask and answer questions.

A: Do you like to swim?
B: No, I don't. Do you like to swim?
A: Yes, I do. I also like to play basketball.
B: Me, too, but I don't like to jump rope.
A: Me, neither.

CONVERSATIONS

A. SUE: Alana, read this ad. The health club wants new members. We can get in shape and meet new friends there.

ALANA: I don't need a health club. I'm not out of shape. I exercise every day. I don't have the time or the money to go to a health club.

SUE: Oh, come on! There's an Open House tonight. We can have fun there. We can look, and we don't need any money! I know that you're not doing anything tonight.

ALANA: OK. You're right. Let's go and see it.

B. TOM: Hi, I'm Tom. I work here at the Fitness Club. This is our weight room. Stan and his wife Antonia are lifting weights. They're in great shape. They lift weights every evening. Do you like to lift weights, Sue?

SUE: No, I don't. It's very hard.

TOM: What kind of exercise do you usually like to do, Alana?

ALANA: I like to watch Mel Turner's exercise show on TV. I exercise with him every day. And I like to ride my bike, too. It's fun and easy.

weight room:

C. TOM: Well, this is the big exercise room. There are exercise classes here all day. We have a lot of exercise bikes, too. Some members are riding now. And here is the swimming pool.

SUE: Look Alana, there's Julia Bradley. She's swimming in the pool.

TOM: Yes, Julia's a new member. A lot of her friends are members of the health club, too. Do you like to play basketball? Julia and her friends play basketball here every week.

ALANA: Great! I love to play basketball. What fun!

exercise bike:

D. TOM: Here's the health food bar. You can have breakfast, lunch, dinner, or a snack here. You can see that a lot of members are sitting at the bar now.

SUE: Hey, isn't that Ted Crampton?

TED: Hi! Don't you think the health club is great! Do you want a drink? They have juice—orange, apple, or grape—and water, of course.

SUE: Yes, I'd like some apple juice. Thank you. How often do you come to the health club, Ted?

TED: Oh, I come every day! I like the Fitness Club.

SUE: Me, too! What do you think, Alana?

ALANA: Good-by TV and hello Fitness Club!!

 EXERCISE 3: *Understanding the Conversations*

Answer the questions.

1. What kind of exercise does Alana like?
2. Who do Alana and Sue know at the Fitness Club?
3. What can you do at the Fitness Club?

EXERCISE 4: *Do You Know How to Swim?*

A. *Write three things you know how to do and three things you don't know how to do on a sheet of paper.*

B. *Choose something you don't know how to do. Find someone who can teach you how to do it. Then find someone you can teach how to do something.*

A: Do you know how to swim?
B: Yes, I do.
A: I don't know how to swim, but I want to learn. Can you teach me?
B: Of course. No problem.

EXERCISE 5: *Food and Drinks*

What food do you eat at breakfast, lunch, and dinner? What do you have as a snack? Do you eat healthy food?

Breakfast _____

Lunch _____

Dinner _____

Snack _____

VOCABULARY

to exercise	ad
to jump (rope)	basketball
to know how	club
to lift (weights)	juice
to see	member
to watch	pool
	room
Expressions	tonight
Me, neither.	TV
Me, too.	water
See you later.	
What fun!	**Fruit**
	apple
a lot of	banana
easy	grape
fun	orange
hard	
healthy	**Meals**
in/out of shape	breakfast
	lunch
What kind of?	dinner
How often?	a snack

WORD FOR WORD

Have

Have means "possession." Use the simple present tense of **have**.

> I **have** a new car.
> I **don't have** time to talk with you.
> I **don't have** the money to go.

Have can also be used in expressions. Then you can use the simple present or the present progressive tense of **have**.

> I'm **having** a good time. I **have** a good time at the health club every evening.
> We're **not having** fun. We **don't have** fun at work.
> He's **having** a hot dog and milk for lunch. He **has** a hot dog and milk for lunch every day.

 EXERCISE 6: *Have a Try!*

*Work with a partner. Ask and answer the questions. Think of the way you use **have**.*

1. Do you have a large family? How many brothers and sisters do you have?
2. What do you like to have for lunch? for breakfast? for dinner?
3. Are you having fun in class today?

G GRAMMAR

A. *Simple Present Tense with Every*

> How often do Mr. and Mrs. Barrett swim?
> They swim **every** morning.
>   **every** Sunday.
>   **every** Friday afternoon.

 EXERCISE 7: *Talk About Your Life*

A. *Write five sentences about yourself on a sheet of paper.*

   I go to English class every day.

1. every morning   3. every week   5. every year
2. every afternoon   4. every day

B. *Work with a partner. Find out what your partner does. Ask and answer questions.*

A: What do you do every morning?
B: I eat a large breakfast. What do you do?
A: I ride my exercise bike.

B. *Simple Present Tense vs. Present Progressive Tense*

Use the simple present tense to talk about things that happen a lot.

> What **do** you **do** on Saturday morning?
> I **ride** my bike.
> Do you **ride** your bike every Saturday?
> Yes, I **do.**

Use the present progressive tense to talk about things that are happening now.

> What **is** Liz **doing** now?
> She**'s riding** her bike.
> **Is** she **riding** in the park?
> Yes, she **is.**

A lot	Now
in the afternoon	this afternoon
on Saturday	today
every week	now

EXERCISE 8: *Yoko's Afternoon Schedule*

A. *Look at Yoko's schedule. Work with a partner. Ask and answer the questions.*

Yoko's Afternoon Schedule						
SUN	MON	TUES	WED	THURS	FRI	SAT
read	do English homework	swim	work in father's office	do English homework	bake a cake	go to the park with friends

1. What does Yoko do every Friday afternoon?
2. When does Yoko do her English homework?
3. Where does Yoko work every Wednesday afternoon?
4. What does Yoko do every Sunday afternoon?
5. When does Yoko swim?
6. What do Yoko and her friends do every Saturday afternoon?

B. *Work with a partner. Ask and answer the questions.*

1. It's Tuesday afternoon. What is Yoko doing?
2. Yoko is baking a cake now. What day is it?
3. It's Monday afternoon. What is Yoko doing?
4. It's Sunday afternoon. What is Yoko doing?
5. Yoko is working in her father's office now. What day is it?

C. *Imperatives*

In the exercise class:
Run. Walk. Don't Stop.

In the classroom:
Listen. Please **sit down. Repeat.**
Don't talk, please. **Raise** your hands.
Close your books, please.

EXERCISE 9: *Who Says What?*

Work with a partner. Who is talking? Who are they talking to? Several answers are possible.

a mother	**a father**
a husband	**a musician**
a spy	**a doctor**
a clerk	**a wife**
a teacher	**a student**
a friend	**a child**

1. Eat a lot of fruit.
2. Eat your food!
3. Don't buy a cake.
4. Exercise every day.
5. Write your answers on a sheet of paper.
6. Fill in the form, please.
7. Don't play my guitar!
8. Don't wear that short skirt.
9. Have a good vacation.
10. Follow that man!

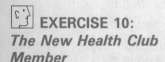 **LISTENING**

Prelistening

Look at the pictures. Where are these people? What do you think they are doing?

1. _____ , _____

4. _____

 EXERCISE 10:
The New Health Club Member

Listen to the conversation. What are the office workers doing now? Write each name under the correct picture.

Richard	**Luis**	**Tony**
Sandra	**Mona**	**Brian**
Harold		

2. _____ , _____

5. _____

3. _____

 PRONUNCIATION

EXERCISE 11: *Like /l/, Right /r/, Window /w/*

Listen and repeat. Listen for the beginning sound in ***like,*** *in* ***right,*** *and in* ***window.***

Like	**Right**	**Window**	**Like**	**Right**	**Window**
let's	raise	word	eleven	address	between
lettuce	read	wife	hello	across	twenty
like	red	white	milk	briefcase	sandwich

EXERCISE 12: *Like /l/ Right /r/ or Window?*

*Listen to each word. Circle **l** if you hear the same beginning sound as in **like**. Circle **r** if you hear the same beginning sound as in **right**. Circle **w** if you hear the same beginning sound as in **window**.*

1.	l	r	w	**6.**	l	r	w
2.	l	r	w	**7.**	l	r	w
3.	l	r	w	**8.**	l	r	w
4.	l	r	w	**9.**	l	r	w
5.	l	r	w	**10.**	l	r	w

SPEAKING

A. You are a reporter. You are writing about health for your newspaper. You want to talk to some people about their ideas. Work with a partner. Find out what he or she thinks about his or her health. Here are some questions you can ask. Think of your own questions, too.

B. Tell the class about your partner.

Do you exercise?
Do you like to exercise?
What kind of exercise do you like to do?
How often do you exercise?
Where do you like to exercise?
Do you like to eat healthy food?
What food do you like to eat?
Do you like to eat a snack between meals? Is this healthy?
What drinks do you like?
Do you read books about health?
Do you watch TV shows about health or exercise?
Do you walk to school or to work?
Do you think you're healthy?
Do you think you're in shape?

READING

Prereading

A. Are you in shape? What do you do to get in shape? Do you have a lot of time to exercise? Does your school have a health program for its students? Do you know any offices that have exercise rooms for the workers?

B. Look at the pictures. Where are the people? What are they doing? Read the title. What do you think **working out** means? What do you think the reading is about?

Working Out At Work

A lot of people are out of shape. They say that they don't have time to exercise or to eat right. For this reason, many companies are now providing exercise centers and health classes for their workers.

5 Workers in both large and small companies can exercise during their lunch hour. For example, at Texas Instruments, Inc., in Dallas, there is an exercise center with fitness instructors and nutrition classes for the 22,000 employees. At one of Nike's locations, there is a weight machine, two
10 exercise bicycles, and two rowing machines for the 300 employees. British Rail at Waterloo Station in London has an exercise room for its employees.

At Bonne Bell in Ohio, employees get thirty extra minutes at lunchtime if they want to exercise. And they can wear
15 exercise clothes at work in the afternoon. If a Bonne Bell employee exercises four days a week for half a year, he or she gets $250 from the company!

It is important to be healthy and in shape. But don't wait for your company or school to start a health program. You can
20 eat right and start your own exercise routine right now.

company: place you work

provide: have

fitness: health

nutrition: healthy eating

employee: worker

rowing machine:

extra: +

half: 1/2

 EXERCISE 13: *Understanding the Reading*

Read the sentence. Circle **T** *for true and* **F** *for false. Explain your answers.*

1. T F Both large and small companies have health programs for their workers.
2. T F Nike employees can get money if they exercise a lot.
3. T F Employees can go to classes on healthy eating at Texas Instruments, Inc.
4. T F You need to wait for your company or school to start a health program.

 WRITING

A. Prewriting. Writing. You are writing a list of ideas for good health. Work with a partner. Write fifteen ideas. Choose ten ideas you like best and write them on a sheet of paper. Write complete sentences.

B. Revising. Presenting. Read the sentences. Is everything correct? Make the corrections. Write the final copy. Tell the class your ideas.

DISCUSSION

1. Do you think health programs for students and workers are good? Explain.

2. Can you be healthy but not exercise? Can you exercise but not be healthy? Explain.

SPEAK OUT!

You and your partner work at a health club. You want new members. Make a TV ad about your club. Then present your ad to the class. (Name your health club. Talk about what you can do there. Tell the hours the club is open. Tell the cost of membership. Tell where the club is.)

UNIT 8 Soap Suds

WARM UP

What are they doing? How do they feel?

EXERCISE 1: *How Do They Feel?*

A. *Look at the pictures. Match each picture with the correct word.*

1. _____   5. _____   **a.** angry   **e.** nervous
2. _____   6. _____   **b.** sad   **f.** happy
3. _____   7. _____   **c.** sick   **g.** shocked
4. _____   8. _____   **d.** worried **h.** tired

B. *Look at the pictures. Work with a partner. Ask and answer questions.*

A: What's she doing?
B: She's eating some cake.
A: How does she feel?
B: She feels happy.

CONVERSATIONS

In the last *Soap Suds* magazine, David and Mona were in love. But today something happened. . . .

SCENE 1

Mona, darling! I can't live without you!

Oh, David, my good friend . . .

SCENE 2

What are you saying? Why did you call me "friend"? I'm your boyfriend. I love you.

I'm sorry, David. Don't be angry with me, but I don't love you.

EXERCISE 2:

Understanding the Conversations

Answer the questions.

1. Does David love Mona?
2. Did Mona love David yesterday?
3. Does Mona love David now?
4. Why is David confused?
5. Do you think Mona and David can be friends?

SCENE 3

Angry? I'm sad, very sad—and shocked. Mona, I don't understand. Just yesterday we danced to our favorite music!

Yes, we did. But I don't love you today. I'm returning your ring.

SCENE 4

Stop, listen to me. . . Mona, is there another man?

I'm sorry David, but there is. I love him now and not you.

SCENE 5

I knew it! But I'm so confused. We were in love. And now you love another man, and I'm alone. I can't stand it! Good-by, Mona.

Oh, David wait! Can't we be friends?

EXERCISE 3: *Vocabulary Check*

A. *Work with a partner. Ask and answer the questions. Use these words. You can answer with more than one word.*

afraid	**great**	**hungry**	**shocked**	**thirsty**
angry	**happy**	**nervous**	**sick**	**tired**
confused	**healthy**	**sad**	**terrible**	**worried**

1. You get a thousand dollars from your friend. How do you feel?
2. You have a test now. How do you feel?
3. You lifted weights for fifty minutes. How do you feel?
4. You're flying a plane for the first time. How do you feel?
5. You want to eat. How do you feel?
6. Your family buys a new house. How do you feel?
7. The baby is crying. How do you feel?

B. *Think of more examples and ask another student questions.*

WORD FOR WORD

Adverbs of Time

Then	Now
yesterday	today
yesterday morning	this morning
yesterday afternoon	this afternoon
yesterday evening	this evening
last night	tonight
last week	this week
last Thursday	Thursday
last year	this year
last month	this month

VOCABULARY

	Pronouns	**Feelings**
to be: was/were		
to call	him	afraid
to cry	me	angry
to laugh	them	confused
to love	us	happy
to return		nervous
to say	home	sad
to smile	homework	shocked
	hour	sick
alone	house	terrible
favorite	minute	worried
in love	ring	
	soap opera	because
Expressions	yesterday	
How do you feel?		How long?
I can't stand it!		Why?

EXERCISE 4: *What Did You Do?*

Work with a partner. What did you do? What did your partner do? Write the verb on the line. Then tell the class.

What did you do . . . . . ?	**I . . .**	**My partner . . .**
1. last night	_____	_____
2. last Monday	_____	_____
3. yesterday afternoon	_____	_____
4. last year	_____	_____
5. last week	_____	_____

GRAMMAR

A. *The Simple Past Tense:*
Yes/No Questions and Short Answers with To Be

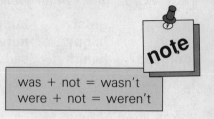

note

was + not = wasn't
were + not = weren't

I/He/She/It **was** not sad.
Was (he) angry?
Yes, (he) **was.**/No, (he) **wasn't.**

You/We/They **were not** at the mall.
Were (they) at the park?
Yes, (they) **were.**/No, (they) **weren't.**

 EXERCISE 5: *Was Your Sister Angry?*

Ask and answer questions.

your sister/angry
A: Was your sister angry yesterday?
B: Yes, she was.

Joe and Sue/in the park
A: Were Joe and Sue in the park yesterday afternoon?
B: No, they weren't. They were at the health club.

Use These Words
yesterday
yesterday morning/afternoon/evening
last night/week/year/Thursday

1. you/nervous
2. your teacher/sick
3. your friend/at school
4. your mother and father/at the theater
5. your books/on the desk
6. your daughter/happy

B. *The Simple Past Tense:*
Information Questions with To Be

Who was angry?
(The boyfriend) **was** angry.
How long **was** (he) angry?
(He) **was** angry for two hours.

Who was confused?
(The students) **were** confused.
(Why) were (they) confused.
Because (they) **were** nervous.

 EXERCISE 6: *What's the Question?*

Write the correct question for each answer.

1. (*Where?*) _____ He was at the mall last night.

2. (*Yes/No?*) _____ No, he wasn't alone.

3. (*Who?*) _____ He was with his wife.

4. (*How long?*) _____ They were at the mall for three hours.

5. (*Yes/No?*) _____ Yes, they were in Style City.

6. (*Why?*) _____ Because they returned a shirt.

C. *The Simple Past Tense:* Yes/No Questions and Short Answers

I/You/He/She/We/They **lifted** weights.
Did (he) **jump** rope?
Yes, (he) **did.**/No, (he) **didn't.**

 EXERCISE 7: *Did You Talk to Your Mother Yesterday?*

Write questions about yesterday on a sheet of paper. Use these verbs. Then ask another student your questions.

talk	Did you talk to your mother yesterday? Yes, I did.
walk	Did you walk in the park yesterday? No, I didn't. I was at home all day.

1. listen to   **3.** study   **5.** cook   **7.** talk
2. work   **4.** exercise   **6.** dance   **8.** play

D. *The Simple Past Tense:* Information Questions

What did you **do** yesterday?	I **watched** a soap opera.
Where did you **watch** it?	At home.
Who did you **watch** it with?	With my mother.
How long did you **watch** it?	We **watched** it for one hour.
When did you **call** Mona?	At eight o'clock.
Why did you **call** her?	**Because** I **needed** to talk to her.

EXERCISE 8: *Mona and David*

Fill in the correct verbs. Use these words. You can use the words more than one time.

did
didn't
play
played
do
study
studied

FRAN: Mona, what **(1)** _____ David **(2)** _____ last Sunday night?

MONA: He **(3)** _____ English at his house.

FRAN: **(4)** _____ you **(5)** _____ with him?

MONA: No, I **(6)** _____ .

FRAN: What did you **(7)** _____ ?

MONA: I **(8)** _____ basketball.

E. *Object Pronouns*

Use object prepositions after verbs and prepositions.

I	**me**	we	**us**
he	**him**	you	**you**
she	**her**	they	**them**
it	**it**		

He loves **me.**
He's angry with **me.**

EXERCISE 9: *Write the Word!*

Write the correct pronoun on the line.

My husband Tony loves the theater. I go with **(1)** _____ every Friday night. Sometimes our daughter and son go with **(2)** _____ to the theater. Sometimes I talk in the theater. My family gets angry with **(3)** _____ and says, ''Be quiet. We're listening to the actors, not to **(4)** _____ .'' But I'm not angry with **(5)** _____ because they're my family.

Then we usually go to our favorite place to eat, Pasta Pronto. We like **(6)** _____ a lot. Everyone there knows **(7)** _____ and says hello. They like our daughter a lot, and they always smile at **(8)** _____ .

LISTENING

Prelistening

Do you watch soap operas on TV? Do you listen to soap operas on the radio? In the United States in the 1940s and 1950s, there were a lot of soap operas on the radio. Are there radio soap operas in your country? What are their names?

EXERCISE 10: *The World Is Small, A Radio Soap Opera*

Read the questions. Listen to the soap opera. Circle the best answer to each question.

1. What is wrong with Maria?
   a. Maria thinks Roberto loves another woman.
   b. Maria thinks Antonio doesn't love her.
   c. Maria thinks she doesn't love Antonio or Roberto.

2. Why didn't Maria talk to Roberto in the park?
   a. Antonio was with her.
   b. She was angry and confused.
   c. She didn't like him.

3. How does Maria feel?
   a. She feels afraid and confused.
   b. She feels alone, but happy.
   c. She feels confused and sad.

PRONUNCIATION

EXERCISE 11: *Is It Past Tense?*

Listen to the verbs. Do you hear a past tense ending? Circle the word you hear.

1. play   played
2. dance   danced
3. wait   waited

4. stop   stopped
5. need   needed
6. exercise   exercised

SPEAKING

Work with a group of people. You are one of the people in a soap opera. Each person in the soap opera has a feeling. Ask each other questions about your feelings. Why does each person feel that way? Make up a story. Then share your ideas with the class.

READING

Prereading

Do you read magazines or newspapers about soap operas? Do you know anyone who reads them? What's in them? Look at the page. What soap opera is the page about?

WHAT HAPPENED IN THE SOAPS LAST WEEK?

Family Trees

MONDAY

Susan didn't work for ten years. Then she wanted to start teaching again. But she thought that Frank, her husband, didn't want her to work. Susan was very sad and confused. She didn't know what to do.

Susan called her friend Angela. She talked to her about her problem. Angela said, ''Follow your heart. You love to teach. Talk to Frank.''

Billy, Susan's son, asked a new girlfriend to go to the mall with him.

again: another time

said: *say* in the past tense

TUESDAY

Billy is having problems in school. Billy's teacher called Susan and said that he didn't study, listen, or do his homework. Susan cried. She was very worried. Susan talked to Billy about school, but he didn't want to talk about it. All he wanted to do was be with his new girlfriend.

Susan waited for Frank to come home. She wanted to talk to him about their son. Frank didn't come home until ten o'clock. Susan was in bed. She didn't talk to him about anything.

WEDNESDAY

Susan talked to Frank in the morning. He called Billy's teacher. At work, Frank asked some men about their wives. A lot of wives worked. He was confused. Their family needed money, but he wanted Susan to be at home. And now Billy needs help.

Susan looked in the newspaper for a job. Billy went to the mall again with his new girlfriend. He didn't study for his test.

help: to do something that is needed

THURSDAY

Read the sentence. Circle **T** for *true* and **F** for *false.* *Explain.*

1. T F Susan works at a school.
2. T F Angela is Billy's girlfriend.
3. T F Susan is worried about her son.
4. T F Frank doesn't want Susan to work.
5. T F Susan's family needs money.

WRITING

A. Prewriting. Writing.
You are a writer for *Soap Summaries.* Look at the pictures. What happened in *Family Trees* on Thursday and on Friday? Write a paragraph about the soap opera using the pictures.

B. Revising. Presenting. Read the paragraph. Is everything correct? Make any corrections. Write the final copy.

THURSDAY

FRIDAY

SPEAK OUT!

Work with a partner. Choose a favorite soap opera or other TV program. Did you watch the show last week? Talk about two people from the show. What happened to them last week? Tell the class.

WARM UP

A. What do you like to do on vacation? Do you like to discover new things? go to interesting places? eat new foods? learn about famous people?

B. Miriam is going on vacation in Mexico. What does she want to do?

1. eat in restaurants

4. climb a mountain

7. go to famous places

2. ride a bike

5. see pyramids

8. take a lot of pictures

3. swim

6. speak Spanish

9. write post cards

EXERCISE 1: *What Did Miriam Do on Vacation?*

Miriam got back from her vacation yesterday. What did she do? Work with a partner. Ask and answer questions.

1. ate
A: Where did Miriam eat?
B: She ate in some good restaurants.

2. rode
3. swam
4. climbed

5. saw
6. spoke
7. went to

8. took
9. wrote

CONVERSATIONS

A. **JOHN:** We need to remember a lot for our ancient history test. Why don't you ask me some questions first? Then I can ask you some questions.

MARK: Fine. Let's see . . . first question. Who wrote *The Iliad*?

JOHN: That's easy. Homer wrote *The Iliad*.

MARK: Second question. What was *The Iliad* about?

JOHN: It was about a war between Greece and Troy.

MARK: Was it about a real war?

JOHN: Yes, it was. For a long time people thought the war didn't really happen. They thought *The Iliad* was just a story. But Heinrich Schliemann read it, and he thought it was true. He looked for the ruins of Troy, and he found them in the 1870s.

MARK: Did the Trojans win the war?

JOHN: No, they didn't. They lost.

B. **JOHN:** OK. Now I want to ask some questions. Who built Stonehenge and when?

MARK: Ancient people of England built it in about 1800 B.C. We don't really know who they were or how they did it. But we know what they did there.

JOHN: What did they do at Stonehenge?

MARK: They watched the sun, the moon, and the stars, and they made a calendar.

C. **JOHN:** All right. Here are the last questions. Where are the ruins of the famous Mayan city of Tikal?

MARK: Oh, that's easy. They're in Guatemala.

JOHN: When did the Mayas live there?

MARK: They started to build stone buildings there in about 900 B.C. They lived there to about A.D. 900.

JOHN: Great! I think we're ready for our test.

ancient: very old

Troy:

Trojans: people from Troy

Stonehenge:

Tikal:

EXERCISE 2: *Understanding the Conversations*

These questions were on John and Mark's history test. Circle the correct answers.

1. What was *The Iliad* about?
   a. a real war
   b. a war that never happened
   c. Heinrich Schliemann's discoveries

2. Who won the Trojan War?
   a. the Trojans
   b. the Greeks
   c. No one. It never happened.

3. Who discovered the ruins of Troy?
   a. Homer
   b. the ancient Greeks
   c. Heinrich Schliemann

4. Where is Stonehenge?
   a. Greece
   b. England
   c. Guatemala

5. Where is Tikal?
   a. Greece
   b. England
   c. Guatemala

6. Who built Tikal?
   a. the Greeks
   b. the Trojans
   c. the Mayas

EXERCISE 3: *Vocabulary Check*

Write the letter of the correct picture on the line.

1. post card _____
2. mountain _____
3. calendar _____
4. moon _____
5. star _____
6. sun _____
7. building _____
8. ruins _____

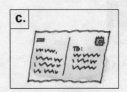

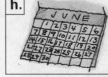

VOCABULARY

New Past Tense Forms
buy/bought
come/came
do/did
eat/ate
get/got
go/went
have/had
make/made
read/read
ride/rode
see/saw
speak/spoke
swim/swam
take/took
think/thought
write/wrote

building
calendar
date
history
moon
mountain
post card
ruins
star
stone
sun
test
war

beautiful
famous
real

second
third

Regular Verbs
climb
discover
learn
look for
remember

Irregular Verbs
build/built
find/found
lose/lost
win/won

Expressions
Why don't you (start)?
When (were) (you) born?

EXERCISE 4: *Same or Opposite?*

*Do these words mean the same or the opposite? Write **S** (same) or **O** (opposite) on the line.*

_____ 1. went   came
_____ 2. found   discovered
_____ 3. built   made

_____ 4. answered   asked
_____ 5. looked at   saw
_____ 6. won   lost

WORD FOR WORD

A. Ordinal Numbers

Cardinal numbers tell how many.
Ordinal numbers tell what's next.

> The building has **thirteen** floors.
> Joe lives on the **thirteenth** floor.

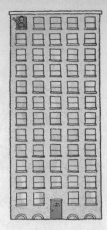

thirteenth (13th)
twelfth (12th)
eleventh (11th)
tenth (10th)
ninth (9th)
eighth (8th)
seventh (7th)
sixth (6th)
fifth (5th)
fourth (4th)
third (3rd)
second (2nd)
first (1st)

B. Dates

> When were you born? I was born on **September fourteenth, 1976.**
> When is your mother's birthday? Her birthday is **July 7th.**

 EXERCISE 5: *Birthdays*

A. *When do you think these famous people were born?*

a. July 24, 1783
b. November 19, 1917
c. July 12, 100 B.C.
d. March 12, 1879

B. *Work with a partner. Compare your answers. Do you agree?*

A: When do you think Albert Einstein was born?
B: I think he was born on March twelfth, eighteen seventy-nine.

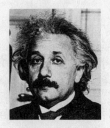

1. Albert Einstein

2. Simón Bolívar

3. Indira Gandhi

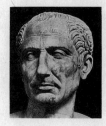

4. Julius Caesar

GRAMMAR

The Simple Past Tense: Irregular Verbs

The past tense of many English verbs is not spelled with **-ed.**

Regular Verbs	Irregular Verbs
(Luis) **studied** last night.	(Carol) **bought** a TV last week.
Did (he) **study** with Mark?	**Did** (she) **buy** it at the mall?
Yes, (he) **did.**/No, (he) **didn't.**	Yes, (she) **did.**/No, (she) **didn't.**
(Where) did they study?	**(Why)** did she **buy** a TV?
They **studied** at Mark's house.	Because she **didn't have** a TV.

EXERCISE 6: *Verb Forms*

Circle the answers.

1. In questions use: **eat**   **ate**   **study**   **studied.**
2. In sentences with *not* use: **eat**   **ate**   **study**   **studied.**
3. In sentences without *not* use: **eat**   **ate**   **study**   **studied.**

EXERCISE 7: *What Did You Do Last Week?*

A. *What did you do last week? Write* **yes** *or* **no** *under* **You.**

B. *Work with a partner. Ask questions. Write* **yes** *or* **no** *under* **Your partner.**

A: Did you buy any new clothes last week?
B: No, I didn't. Did you buy any new clothes last week?
A: Yes, I did.

	You	Your Partner
1. bought some new clothes	___	___
2. cooked dinner	___	___
3. had a test	___	___
4. listened to music	___	___
5. rode a bike	___	___
6. studied English	___	___
7. swam	___	___
8. went to a mall	___	___

EXERCISE 8: *What Did Tom Do Last Week?*

Work with a partner. What did Tom do last week? Ask and answer questions. One partner looks at Calendar A. The other partner looks at Calendar B on page 76. Fill in Tom's calendar.

A: What did Tom do on Monday?
B: He bought new pants.

Calendar A

MON.	_____
TUES.	got an interesting post card from a friend
WED.	_____
THURS.	spoke with his teacher about the test
FRI.	_____
SAT.	looked for a new jacket at the mall
SUN.	_____

LISTENING

Prelistening

A. What interesting places do you know about? Where did you learn about them?

B. Do you know these places? What do you know about them?

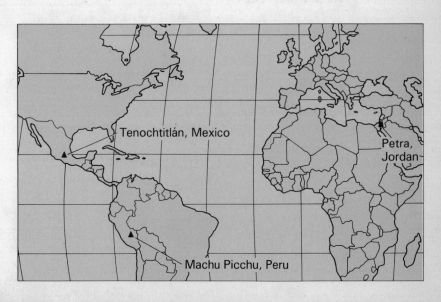

Tenochtitlán, Mexico

Petra, Jordan

Machu Picchu, Peru

EXERCISE 9: *What Did You Learn?*

*Listen to the conversation.
What did the students learn
about these people? Write
an* **X**.

1. had houses with one room

2. had buildings of red stone

3. had buildings of white stone

4. wrote with pictures

5. lived in the mountains

	Nabateans	Incas	Aztecs

 PRONUNCIATION

EXERCISE 10: *Think /θ/*

Listen and repeat.

1. thanks
2. third
3. Thursday
4. three
5. thought
6. birthday
7. healthy
8. month
9. thirteenth
10. twentieth

EXERCISE 11: *Do You Hear It?*

Listen to the words. Some have the same beginning sound as
think *and others don't. Write* **yes** *when you hear the
beginning sound of* **think** *and* **no** *when you don't.*

1. _____
2. _____
3. _____
4. _____
5. _____
6. _____
7. _____
8. _____

 SPEAKING

You need to complete a time
line for a test on famous
people. Work with a partner.
One partner looks at Time
Line A. The other looks at
Time Line B on page 76. Ask
questions to find out the
information you don't have.

A: Why don't you ask me the
   first question?
B: OK. What did Henry Ford
   make?
A: He made his first car.
B: When did he make it?
A: He made it in 1893.

Time Line A	
1600	Shakespeare wrote _____ .
1893	Henry Ford made his first car.
	_____ found ruins on Crete, Greece.
1926	Gertrude Ederle swam the English Channel.
	Walt Disney _____ .
1969	Neil Armstrong walked on the moon.
	Mark Spitz won _____ .
1975	Mrs. Junko Tabei climbed Mount Everest.

 READING

Prereading

Look at the picture. Do you know about this place? Where is it?

Hiram Bingham and the Lost City of Machu Picchu

Hiram Bingham (1875–1956) was a history teacher. He wanted to learn about the ancient people of South America. He visited South America five times and discovered many ancient ruins. His most famous discovery was in Peru. It was
5 the ruins of Machu Picchu, the lost city of the Incas.

The Incas lived in South America for three hundred years. Then, in the 1500s, they lost a war with the Spanish. The Spanish tried to destroy everything that the Incas built, but people said there was still an old city somewhere in the
10 mountains.

Many people searched for Machu Picchu, but no one found it. Then, in 1911, Bingham learned about some ruins on a mountain next to the Urubamba River. Bingham climbed the mountain, and there was the city!

15 At one time, a thousand people lived in Machu Picchu. They built long streets and beautiful stone buildings. One building was an observatory where they watched the sun, moon, and stars. They told time by the stars and made a calendar to mark the hours, days, and years.

20 When did these people leave Machu Picchu? Where did they go? No one knows.

Today tourists can take buses up to these famous ruins. They walk on the streets and take pictures of the houses. They like being in this ancient place.

destroy: make into ruins
still: at that time

told time: learned what time

 EXERCISE 12: *Getting Meaning from Context*

Find the word in the the reading. Circle the answer that means the same.

1. visited (*line 3*)	**a.** read about	**b.** looked for	**c.** went to
2. lost (*line 5*)	**a.** not won	**b.** not found	**c.** old
3. searched for (*line 11*)	**a.** talked about	**b.** saw	**c.** looked for
4. tourists (*line 22*)	**a.** people on business	**b.** people on vacation	**c.** bus drivers
5. up (*line 22*)	**a.** ↓	**b.** ↑	**c.** ←

WRITING

A. Prewriting. Fill in the time line of your life. Answer these questions. Think of other questions and answer them, too.

Where were you born? When?
Where did you live? When?
What important things happened to you? When?
What interesting people did you meet? When?
What did you learn how to do? When?

B. Writing. Write five sentences about your life. Use information from the time line.

C. Revising. Presenting. Read your sentences. Is everything correct? Make any corrections. Write the final copy.

Time Line of Your Life

Born . . .	
Now	

SPEAK OUT!

Work with a partner. Take turns asking each other the questions in the Writing section. Then tell the class about your partner.

Calendar B

MON.	bought new pants
TUES.	_____
WED.	had a history test
THURS.	_____
FRI.	wrote a long letter to a friend
SAT.	_____
SUN.	played basketball with his friends

Time Line B	
1600	Shakespeare wrote *Twelfth Night*.
	Henry Ford made _____ .
1900	Sir Arthur Evans found ruins on Crete, Greece.
	Gertrude Ederle _____ .
1955	Walt Disney opened Disneyland.
	_____ walked on the moon.
1972	Mark Spitz won seven gold medals in the Olympics.
	Mrs. Junko Tabei climbed _____ .

UNIT 10 What's Your Opinion?

 WARM UP

A. There are a lot of ads in newspapers, in magazines, and on TV. Do you read or listen to the ads? What kinds of information do you find in ads?

B. Read these ads. Do they answer questions with **who, what, when,** and **where?**

Do you want to get in shape and be thin? Come to **L.A. Health Club.** Say good-by to your fat! We have early morning classes. Come in for one free class!

ADDRESS: 1410 Lake Avenue

PHONE: (708) 375-0909

Shoe City is having a sale! Saturday 10 A.M. to 10:00 P.M. Come early or late, but come!
165 Green Street

(815) 354-6677

DERMIT'S LANGUAGE SCHOOL

We can teach you to speak Spanish, French, Italian, German, Russian, Arabic, or Japanese. We have classes for adults and children. We have classes in the morning, afternoon, and evening, and on the weekend.

CALL TODAY.

Our phone number is (708) 375-7676.
Or come to our office at 675 Park Street.

Do you want a good job? Study at Robert's Secretarial School. We can teach you to type in one day! Don't wait! Call for an interview any day before 9 P.M. We're at 1946 Park Street. Our telephone number is (708) 375-0700.

Cooper's Baby Food on sale today at City Market, 927 Green Street. Open every day from 7 A.M. to 10 P.M.
Phone (708) 375-8976.

Are you tall?
Do you need to wear big clothes? Come to Highland's Big and Tall Men's Store. SALE THIS WEEKEND on all pants!
250 Mountain View Road
(815) 354-6057

Do you need someone to clean your house? CALL MRS. CLEAN. Our people can clean anything and they can come anytime. Call us today at (815) 354-2441 and have a clean house tonight!
367 MOUNTAIN VIEW ROAD

We want you to be our reporters! Tell us what's happening in the city. Call us at (708) 375-7575 with your news. We're here every day, 24 hours a day.
WNTC Radio **1232 Lake Avenue**

 EXERCISE 1: *What? When? Where?*

*Look at the ads. Work with a partner. Ask and answer questions about them with **what, when,** and **where.***

A: What does Robert's Secretarial School teach you to do?
B: Type.
A: When can I call?
B: Every day before nine P.M.
A: Where is the school?
B: It's on Park Street.

UNIT 10 WHAT'S YOUR OPINION?

EXERCISE 2: *Where Can You Go? Who Can You Call?*

Answer the questions about the ads on page 77.

1. Your father is very tall. You want to buy some pants for his birthday. Where can you go?
2. Your mother wants you to buy some food for the baby. Where can you go?
3. You want your son to learn Italian. Where can he go?
4. Your house is dirty. You don't have time to clean it. You want someone to clean it for you. Who can you call?
5. You want to teach people to be healthy. Where can you look for a job?
6. You and your friends saw a famous actor at the airport. You think this is interesting news. Who can you call?

CONVERSATIONS

A. **REPORTER:** Good afternoon. I'm Doug Lee. Welcome to *Person on the Street.* Every week I ask people questions. I find out their opinions about something in the news. Excuse me, ma'am. I'd like to ask you a question.

WOMAN 1: All right. What is it?

REPORTER: The city wants to build a new office building next to the park. What do you think about it?

WOMAN 1: Oh, I saw the design for that on TV. It's a tall, ugly building. I don't want the city to build it.

REPORTER: How about you, sir? What do you think?

MAN 1: I agree with her. I don't want them to build it next to our pretty park. They're making a big mistake.

REPORTER: And you, miss? What's your opinion?

WOMAN 2: Well, I think the building is a good idea. We need new business to come to our city, and a lot of people like to work in a new building. I agree with the city.

REPORTER: Thank you very much.

B. **REPORTER:** Now, for my second question. Excuse me, ma'am. City High School said that they didn't have money, and they stopped all music classes. What do you think about that?

WOMAN 3: Well, I was shocked and angry! I didn't want the school to stop the music classes. My child loved them.

REPORTER: And you, sir? What do you think?

MAN 2: I disagree with her. The school needed to stop some classes. And students don't need to learn music!

REPORTER: Thank you very much. That's my report for today. See you next week.

EXERCISE 3:
Understanding the Conversations

Answer the questions in complete sentences.

1. What does the city want to do?
2. Which people agree with the city? Explain why.
3. Which people disagree with the city? Explain why.
4. What did the high school do?
5. Who didn't agree with the high school? Explain why.

 EXERCISE 4: *Opposites*

Happy and ***sad*** are opposites. Write the opposite for each word.

1. small _____

2. early _____

3. short _____

4. agree _____

5. clean _____

6. pretty _____

7. thin _____

8. baby _____

VOCABULARY

adult	big
article	clean
baby	dirty
information	fat
interview	free
job	pretty
opinion	tall
the news	thin
radio	ugly
report	
telephone/phone	to agree
weekend	to clean
	to disagree
early	to find out/found out
here	to make a mistake
late	to tell/told
more	

Expressions
All right.
Would you like . . . ?

WORD FOR WORD

A. *Phone Numbers*

These are North American phone numbers. Say them like this.

(219) 725-3363
area code two-one-nine, seven-two-five, three-three-six-three

555-0900
five-five-five, oh-nine hundred

555 - 8347

B. *Addresses*

Say addresses like this.

250 Park Avenue = two-fifty Park Avenue
1456 Green Street = fourteen-fifty-six Green Street
2019 Mountain View Road = twenty-nineteen Mountain View Road

EXERCISE 5: *Addresses and Phone Numbers*

Work with a partner. Ask and answer questions about the ads on page 77.

A: I want to study typing. Where can I go?
B: Go to Robert's Secretarial School.
A: What's the address?
B: It's nineteen-forty-six Park Street.
A: And the phone number?
B: Area code seven-oh-eight, three-seven-five, oh-seven hundred.
A: Thanks.
B: You're welcome.

1. to learn Italian
2. to lose some weight
3. to buy some shoes
4. to buy some big clothes
5. to find someone to clean my house
6. to buy some baby food
7. to get in shape
8. to report some news

GRAMMAR

Verb Complementation

With some verbs, we use an infinitive after the object.

WANT	What do you **want me to do** now? I **want you to read** this report.
TELL	Did Mariko **tell you to buy** a newspaper? Yes. She **told me to buy** a *Chicago Star*.
TEACH	Did Sylvia **teach Bill to swim**? Yes, she did. She **taught him to swim** yesterday.
ASK	Please **ask your mother to call** me.
NEED	Do they **need someone to go** to the store now? Yes, they do.
WOULD LIKE	Where **would** you **like me to buy** the shirt? **I'd like you to buy** the shirt at Style City.

EXERCISE 6: *My Mother Wants Me To Make Dinner!*

A. *Write eight sentences on a sheet of paper. Choose items from each section of the box or make up some of your own.*

B. *Read your partner's sentences. Are they the same as your sentences?*

My mother	want/wants	me	to clean (my) room.
My sister	asked		to close the door.
My brothers	need/needs		to type a letter for (her).
My doctor	is/are teaching		to swim.
My friends	told		to make dinner.
My teacher			to be happy.
_____			_____

EXERCISE 7:

What Do They Want Them to Do?

A. *Work with a partner. Look at the pictures. Ask and answer questions about the pictures.*

A: What does she want him to do?

B: She wants him to be thin.

B. *Look at the pictures again. Write the questions and answers on a sheet of paper.*

LISTENING

Prelistening

There are many kinds of news shows on the radio and TV. One kind is the talk show. People talk about their opinions of something in the news. Do you listen to talk shows?

EXERCISE 8:

What's Your Opinion?

A. *A headline tells what a news story is about. Listen to the talk show, "What's Your Opinion?" What are the people talking about? Circle the headlines.*

People Disagree About Money for Schools

CITY HAS NO MONEY TO BUILD NEW BUILDING

NO MORE CITY MONEY FOR FREE CONCERTS

CITY STREETS ARE DIRTY!

B. *Listen again and fill in the chart.*

	City's Opinion	Gloria's Opinion	Peter's Opinion
First Problem			
Second Problem			

PRONUNCIATION

EXERCISE 9: *Baby /b/, Very /v/*

Listen and repeat.

Baby	**Very**
big	**v**acation
basket**b**all	**V**enezuela
clu**b**	dri**v**e
jo**b**	ha**v**e
neigh**b**or	disco**v**er
remem**b**er	inter**v**iew

EXERCISE 10: *Which Sound Do You Hear?*

Listen to the word. If you hear the beginning sound of **baby***, write an* **X** *under* **baby***. If you hear the beginning sound of* **very***, write an* **X** *under* **very***.*

	Baby	Very		Baby	Very
1.	_____	_____	6.	_____	_____
2.	_____	_____	7.	_____	_____
3.	_____	_____	8.	_____	_____
4.	_____	_____	9.	_____	_____
5.	_____	_____	10.	_____	_____

SPEAKING

Work with a partner. One partner asks questions to find out the information in 1–4. The other partner looks at the ads on page 77 to answer. Then change roles for 5–8.

Useful Language
Where can I . . . ?
When can I . . . ?
What's the (address)?
Who has . . . ?

1. You want to take Arabic lessons.
   name of school? / address? / phone number?

2. You want to buy some Cooper's Baby Food on sale.
   place? / address?

3. You want to go to the sale at Highland's Big and Tall Men's Store.
   days of sale? / phone number?

4. You want to talk to someone at WNTC Radio.
   phone number? / time? / address?

5. You need to call Mrs. Clean to get someone to clean your house.
   phone number? / time?

6. You want an interview at Robert's Secretarial School.
   phone number? / address? / time?

7. You want to take a free exercise class.
   place? / address? / time?

8. You want to buy some shoes. You don't have a lot of money.
   You need to go to a sale.
   place? / time? / address?

READING

Prereading

Do you like to read newspapers?
What kind of information do
you find in a newspaper article?
What questions does a
newspaper article answer?

EXERCISE 11:
Newspaper Articles

*These newspaper articles are
not in order. Match the parts.
Which parts come first?
second? Write the letters
of the correct paragraphs
under the headlines.*

a.
On Tuesday, he swam at his hotel and then ate lunch at his sister's new health food restaurant, Mary's Cafe. Today he returns to Washington.

b.
In the afternoon, he went to Gregory's Cake Shop on Green Street. He taught people to make his world-famous Franklin's Bittersweet Chocolate Cake. They learned all his secrets. Today he is on The Cook's Corner on TV.

c.
Last year a group of students from City High School went to Spain to study for six months. Now a group of students from Spain is going to study at City High School for six months. Yesterday they went to the school and met with students and teachers.

d.
Sam Franklin's tenth cookbook came out yesterday in bookstores all over the city. In the morning the famous cookbook writer spoke at Bock's Bookstore about health and food. More than one hundred people came to listen and learn.

e.
One Spanish student said, "I think it's a good idea to see other places and get to know other people. I want the students here to learn about us." A City High School student said, "I had a great time in Spain last year. I found out a lot of information about Spain and its people, and I am happy the Spanish students are here."

f.
President Erikson started his new diet and exercise routine this week while on vacation in Vermont. On Monday, he rode his bike for 20 kilometers in the beautiful Green Mountains. He then ate dinner at the hotel.

1. President Gets in Shape

FIRST: _____

SECOND: _____

2. Spanish Students Come to City

FIRST: _____

SECOND: _____

3. Famous Cook Comes to City

FIRST: _____

SECOND: _____

WRITING

News reporters answer four questions in every article: **Who?**
What? Where? When? All the answers can be in one
sentence.

Professor Ames discovered an ancient Incan city in Peru yesterday.
Who did something?   Professor Ames.
What did he or she do?   Discovered an ancient Incan city.
Where did he or she do it? In Peru.
When did he or she do it? Yesterday.

A. Model. Look at the articles you matched in the Reading.
Write the answers to the questions.

	ARTICLE 1	ARTICLE 2	ARTICLE 3
Who?	_____	_____	_____
What?	_____	_____	_____
Where?	_____	_____	_____
When?	_____	_____	_____

B. Prewriting. Writing. You are a reporter for your school
newspaper. Write about something that happened in your class.
Be sure to answer the questions **Who? What? Where?** and
When?

C. Revising. Presenting. Read your article. Is everything
correct? Make any corrections. Write the final copy.

 SPEAK OUT!

Think about a TV show you saw last week. Work with a
partner. Find out about your partner's show. Ask questions
with **who, what, when,** and **where.** Then find out your
partner's opinion. Did he or she like it? What did he or she like
about it? Did you see the show? Do you agree with your
partner's opinion? Tell the class.

WARM UP

What is going to happen in the future? People like to guess. People try to predict the future in many ways.

EXERCISE 1: *Horoscope*

Work with a partner. What is your partner's star sign? What does the horoscope predict about your partner?

A: When's your birthday?
B: August 11th.
A: Then you're a Leo. It says you're going to climb a mountain soon.

DISCUSSION

1. Who have the same star sign? Do they think their horoscope prediction is correct?

2. Do you believe in horoscope predictions? Why or why not?

TODAY'S HOROSCOPE PREDICTIONS FOR THE STAR SIGNS

Aquarius (January 20-February 18): You are going to meet a new friend.

Pisces (February 19-March 20): You are going to get a nice letter.

Aries (March 21-April 19): You are going to meet a famous actress.

Taurus (April 20-May 20): You are going to fall in love soon and get married.

Gemini (May 21-June 21): You are going to meet a famous scientist.

Cancer (June 22-July 22): You are going to say "good-by" to a friend.

Leo (July 23-August 22): You are going to climb a tall mountain soon.

Virgo (August 23-September 22): You are going to go on a vacation soon.

Libra (September 23-October 23): You are going to win a lot of money.

Scorpio (October 24-November 21): You are going to hear some good news.

Sagittarius (November 22-December 21): You are going to talk to an old friend from the past.

Capricorn (December 22-January 19): You are going to find something nice.

EXERCISE 2: *Weather Predictions*

Every day reporters on TV make predictions about the weather. Work with a partner. Look at the map. It's January 25th. Make some predictions about the weather.

A: What's the weather going to be like in Chicago tomorrow?
B: It's going to be cold and windy.

"Today's Weather Report . . . "

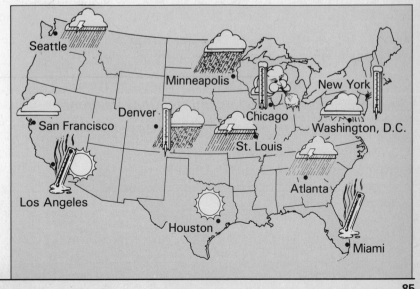

CONVERSATIONS

A. **JESSIE:** Where's the newspaper? I want to read my horoscope for today.

SUKI: It's under my desk.

B. **SUKI:** What does your horoscope say?

JESSIE: It says that I'm going to meet a famous scientist.

SUKI: What about me?

JESSIE: When were you born?

SUKI: September 19th. I'm a Virgo.

JESSIE: The horoscope predicts that you are going to go on a vacation soon.

SUKI: That's amazing! Dan and I are going to visit our parents in Hawaii next weekend.

C. **CHARLIE:** Hi, girls! What's new?

JESSIE: Charlie, listen. Suki's horoscope says she is going to go on a vacation soon, and it's true. She and Dan are going to visit their parents in Hawaii.

CHARLIE: You don't really believe in horoscopes, do you? They're not very scientific.

SUKI: What do you know? Are you some kind of scientist or something?

JESSIE: Why, yes he is. I remember. You're the school's "Scientist of the Year." You wrote a report about the Hubble telescope, didn't you Charlie? It's different from any other telescope, isn't it? It's going to go around the Earth. Didn't you write that it's going to be able to see all the stars?

CHARLIE: That's right. The telescope went into space on April 25th, 1990. It's flying around the earth right now.

SUKI: You see, it's true. Jessie's horoscope prediction was right, too! She did meet a famous scientist today.

EXERCISE 3: *Understanding the Conversations*

Answer the question in complete sentences.

1. What is going to happen to Suki?
2. What is going to happen to Jessie?
3. Look at the horoscope predictions in Exercise 1. What is Jessie's star sign?
4. Who believes in horoscope readings? Who doesn't?
5. Why does Charlie know about the Hubble telescope?

EXERCISE 4: *Understanding Vocabulary*

Look at the words in the list.
Write the letter of the correct
picture next to each word.

1. _____ cold
2. _____ windy
3. _____ clear
4. _____ hot
5. _____ cloudy
6. _____ rainy
7. _____ sunny
8. _____ snowy

VOCABULARY

Earth	to be able (to do something)
future	to believe
horoscope	to get/got married
past	to guess
scientist	to predict
space	
telescope	soon
	tomorrow
Weather	around
clear	down
cloudy	over
cold	under
hot	up
rainy/rain	different (from)
snowy/snow	the same (as)
sunny	
windy	***Expressions***
	What's the weather like?
	That's amazing!

 WORD FOR WORD

Up, Down, Around, Over, Under

Up, down, around, over, and **under** are
prepositions that tell which way.

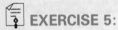 **EXERCISE 5:**
King Kong Climbs a Tall Building

Look at the picture. Write sentences about
the picture on a sheet of paper. Use
up, down, over, around, and **under.**

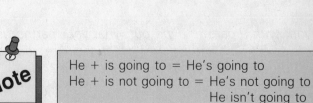

 GRAMMAR

A. *The Future Tense with Going To*

I **am not going to exercise** tonight.

He/She/It **is going to want to
exercise** tomorrow.

You/We/They **are going to be able
to swim** next week.

 note

He + is going to = He's going to
He + is not going to = He's not going to
He isn't going to

EXERCISE 6: *Making Predictions from a Graph*

You can use information about the past to make predictions about the future. This year, people bought a lot of books from Kramer's Bookstore. They are going to buy about the same number of books next year.

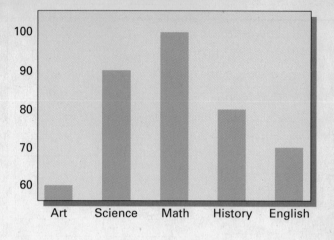

Make predictions about next year. Answer the questions on a sheet of paper. Use complete sentences.

1. What kind of books are people going to buy a lot of next year?
2. About how many history books are people going to buy next year?
3. About how many art books are they going to buy?
4. About how many science books are they going to buy?
5. About how many English books are they going to buy?

EXERCISE 7: *What Are They Going to Do?*

Work with a partner. Read each sentence. What do you think these people are going to do?

A: Susan has a new car.
B: Oh really? What's she going to do?
A: She's going to drive it to California.

1. Tom just won $5,000.
2. Frank loves Isabel.
3. Ed and Carol have a test tomorrow.
4. Cindy is carrying a suitcase.
5. The Smiths are on vacation in Peru.
6. Jason's room is dirty.

EXERCISE 8: *Predicting Your Future*

A. Make predictions about your life. What are you going to be able to do at these times in the future? Write your answers on a sheet of paper.

in two months
In two months, I'm going to be able to go on vacation.

1. tomorrow   **3.** next week   **5.** next year
2. on Saturday   **4.** in six months

B. Work with a partner. Find out what your partner is going to be able to do. Ask and answer questions. Are you going to be able to do the same things? different things?

B. *The Future Tense: Questions*

Is (Joe) **going to play** basketball tonight?
Yes, (he) **is.**/No, **(he's) not.**/No, (he) **isn't.**

Are they **going to win** tomorrow?
Yes, they **are.**/No, **they're not.**/No, they **aren't.**

What is Judy **going to be able to do** next week?
Judy **is going to be able to drive** a car next week.
Who is Judy **going to drive** with?
She **is going to drive** with her teacher.
Where are they **going to drive?**
They **are going to drive** to the mall.

 EXERCISE 9: *Guess the City*

*Work with a partner. Look at the map in the Warm Up on page 85. Choose a city to visit tomorrow. Don't tell your partner. Your partner is going to ask **yes/no** questions about the weather and then guess the city.*

A: Is the weather going to be hot?
B: No, it isn't.
A: Is it going to be windy?
B: Yes, it is.
A: Are you going to go to Chicago?
B: Yes, I am.

EXERCISE 10: *Information Questions*

A. *Each of these people is going to go somewhere tomorrow. Read the cues. Work with a partner. Ask and answer questions about tomorrow.*

Maria and Jeff:
school / eight o'clock in the morning

A: **Where** are Maria and Jeff going to go tomorrow?
B: They're going to go to school tomorrow.
A: **What time** are they going to go to school?
B: They're going to go to school at eight o'clock in the morning.

1. **Bruce:** the office / nine o'clock in the morning
2. **Magda:** the airport / one o'clock in the afternoon
3. **Joe and Pedro:** the store / four o'clock in the afternoon
4. **Anna and Karen:** the health club / seven o'clock in the evening

B. *Now make predictions. What is each person going to do?*

A: **What** are Maria and Jeff going to do tomorrow?
B: They're going to study.

 LISTENING

Prelistening

Do you ever listen to weather reports? What does a weather report tell you?

"Today's Weather Report..."

EXERCISE 11: *Getting Information From a Weather Report*

Listen to the weather report. Fill in the chart with the weather information you hear. Listen to the weather report again to check your answers.

	FRIDAY	SATURDAY	SUNDAY
Los Angeles	morning:	morning:	morning:
	afternoon:	afternoon:	afternoon:
	evening:	evening:	evening:
Mountains		morning:	morning:
		afternoon:	afternoon:
		evening:	evening:

 # PRONUNCIATION

EXERCISE 12: *Yellow /y/, Juice /j/*

Listen to the words. Circle **y** if you hear the same beginning sound as in **yellow**. Circle **j** if you hear the same beginning sound as in **juice**.

1. y j   **5.** y j   **8.** y j
2. y j   **6.** y j   **9.** y j
3. y j   **7.** y j   **10.** y j
4. y j

EXERCISE 13: *Just For Fun*

Listen to these sentences and then practice saying them.

1. Judy buys a yellow jacket every year in June.
2. Jane and Yolanda jumped rope for a long time yesterday.
3. Yes, I know you wear jeans to your job in July.

 # SPEAKING

Mary Ann and Kevin are going to go to the health club at the same time tomorrow morning. Are they going to meet each other there? When do you think they are going to meet each other?

Work with a partner. One person looks at Mary Ann's schedule. The other looks at Kevin's schedule on page 92. Ask and answer questions.

A: What is Kevin going to do first?
B: He's going to play basketball first. Is Mary Ann going to play basketball at 9:00, too?
A: No, she isn't. She's going to go to an exercise class.

Mary Ann's Schedule	
9:00-9:30	go to an exercise class
9:30-9:45	ride an exercise bike
9:45-10:00	lift weights
10:00-10:30	swim in the pool
10:30-10:45	have a snack
10:45-11:00	run

READING

Prereading

Question: What is the same size as a bus, costs $1,500,000,000, and took fifteen years to build?
Answer: The Hubble Telescope

size: how big something is

cost: the money you need to buy something

Looking into Space

On April 25, 1990, the space shuttle *Discovery* took the Hubble telescope into space. The telescope is now 368 miles above the Earth. For the next fifteen years the Hubble telescope is going to look at the planets and stars. Scientists around the world are very interested in the information they are going to be able to get from the telescope because it is going to be able to see more stars, planets, and galaxies than any other telescope before it.

Scientists want to learn more about the universe. With the Hubble telescope, scientists are going to be able to see star light that began to travel to Earth 14 billion years ago. They are going to be able to look into the past and see what happened in space. With this information scientists are going to be able to make predictions about things that are going to happen in space in the future.

Scientists are also going to be able to look for other planets and stars. Is there a planet in the universe that is the same as Earth? The Hubble telescope isn't going to be able to answer *all* the questions scientists have, but it is going to be able to answer a lot of them.

above: over

planet: things in space like Earth
galaxy: a group of stars
universe: all the things in space

EXERCISE 14: *Understanding the Reading*

*Read the sentence. Circle **T** for **true** or **F** for **false**. Explain.*

1. T F The shuttle Discovery is going to take the Hubble into space soon.
2. T F The Hubble is in space 308 miles above the Earth.
3. T F The Hubble telescope sees more than any other telescope.
4. T F Scientists are going to be able to make predictions with the information from the Hubble telescope.
5. T F The telescope is going to be able to see into the past.
6. T F The telescope is going to be able to answer all of the scientists' questions.

DISCUSSION

The Hubble telescope cost $1.5 billion to build. Do you think it's good to use a lot of money for a telescope? Why or why not?

WRITING

A. Prewriting. What are you going to do during the next twenty years? Write your ideas on a sheet of paper. Choose the best ideas.

B. Writing. Then use your list to write a short paragraph about your life in the future.

C. Revising. Presenting. Read the paragraph. Is everything correct? Make the corrections. Write the final copy.

 SPEAK OUT!

Work with a small group. Talk about your future. How many people in your group are going to do each of these things in the next ten years? Fill in the graph. Then talk to the other groups and complete the graph for everyone in the class. How many are going to write a book? How many are going to get married? How many are going to be famous actors/actresses?

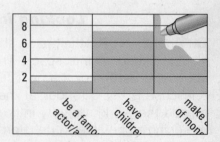

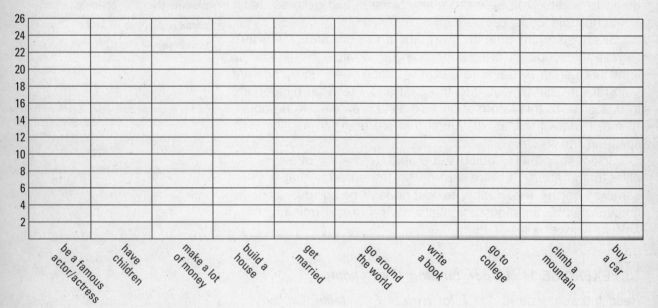

Kevin's Schedule	
9:00-9:30	play basketball
9:30-9:45	run
9:45-10:00	ride an exercise bike
10:00-10:30	swim in the pool
10:30-10:45	lift weights
10:45-11:15	go to an exercise class

UNIT 12 Who's Who?

WARM UP

You are going to a strange city on business. Two people are going to meet you at the airport. You don't know the people, but you have their descriptions. Which of these people are going to meet you?

Kate Brown is an adult female. She is thirty years old. She is five feet seven inches tall. She has blond hair and green eyes. Her hair is long and straight. She's thin, and she wears glasses.

Person _____

Andrew Todd is an adult male. He is twenty years old. He is six feet tall. He has brown hair and brown eyes. His hair is long and curly. He has a big nose and a small mouth.

Person _____

EXERCISE 1: *Guess Who!*

Describe one of the people to your partner. Can your partner guess who?

A: This person is a male.
B: Is he person E?
A: No, he's not. He has brown eyes.
B: Is he person C?
A: No, he has black hair.
B: Is he person B?
A: Yes, he is.

CONVERSATIONS

A. **DETECTIVE ADAMS:**   Tell me what happened.

MARY GREEN: I went to bed at ten o'clock, and at about midnight I heard something. I turned on the light, and I saw my money box on the chair. It was so strange. I know I put it on the table yesterday. When I opened the box, I discovered that all of my money was missing. Then I called the police.

DETECTIVE ADAMS: Did you see anyone?

MARY GREEN: Yes, I saw someone climb out of the window.

DETECTIVE ADAMS: Did you run after the person?

MARY GREEN: No! I was too afraid.

B. **DETECTIVE ADAMS:**   Can you describe the person, Ms. Green?

MARY GREEN: Oh, I don't remember much about him.

DETECTIVE ADAMS: You said ''him.'' Was the person a male?

MARY GREEN: I think so. He had very short hair, and he wore pants and a jacket.

DETECTIVE ADAMS: Was he young?

MARY GREEN: Yes—about 21 or 22.

DETECTIVE ADAMS: What color was his hair?

MARY GREEN: It was blond, and it was straight.

DETECTIVE ADAMS: How about his eyes?

MARY GREEN: I don't know. I didn't see much of his face.

DETECTIVE ADAMS: Was he tall?

MARY GREEN: No, he was short, about 5 feet 6 inches tall.

DETECTIVE ADAMS: Was he thin?

MARY GREEN: Yes, I think so. He climbed out that little window.

DETECTIVE ADAMS: Did he take any of your things?

MARY GREEN: No, I don't think so. Only the money is missing.

DETECTIVE ADAMS: Well, Ms. Green, you remembered a lot. With these clues, we can begin to look for the suspect.

MARY GREEN: Good. I want you to find him soon!

EXERCISE 2: *Comprehension Check*

Answer the questions.

1. What did the suspect take?
2. What time did Mary Green hear him?
3. Where was the box?
4. How did Mary feel?
5. Describe the suspect.

UNIT 12   WHO'S WHO?

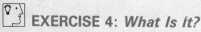

EXERCISE 3: *Opposites*

Write the letter of the word that means the opposite.

1. straight _____
2. ugly _____
3. everyone _____
4. old _____
5. big _____
6. female _____

a. young
b. male
c. curly
d. no one
e. handsome
f. little

EXERCISE 4: *What Is It?*

Write the letter of the word that answers the clue.

1. You turn it on or off. _____
2. You sit on it. _____
3. You see with them. _____
4. You hear with them. _____
5. You smell with it. _____
6. You eat with it. _____

a. nose
b. ears
c. chair
d. mouth
e. light
f. eyes

WORD FOR WORD

Someone, Anyone, Everyone, and No one

Someone, anyone, everyone, and ***no one*** are singular.

> **Is anyone** in the car?
> Yes, I see **someone.** She's wearing glasses.
>
> **Is anyone** in the house?
> No, **no one is** there.
>
> **Was anyone** at the health club?
> Yes, **everyone** in my family **was** there.

EXERCISE 5: *Our Class*

*Write **someone, anyone, everyone,** or **no one** on the line.*

A: Does **(1)** _____ in your class speak English?

B: Of course! **(2)** _____ speaks English. All of us speak English every day.

A: Does **(3)** _____ in your class have blond hair?

B: No, **(4)** _____ does. We all have brown hair.

A: Does **(5)** _____ turn off the light after class?

B: Yes, **(6)** _____ turns off the light after every class.

G GRAMMAR

A. Adjective Review

We use adjectives to
describe people, places, or
things. Adjectives come
before nouns or after **to be**.

> Jeff is **young**. He has **brown** hair. It's **short** and **curly**.
> New York City is a **big** city. It has many **famous** buildings.
> Maria has a **new** table. It's **long**.

EXERCISE 6: *Describing a Suspect*

*Look at the picture. The man with the briefcase took some
important books. Work with a partner. One of you is a
detective. The other one of you saw him leave the office. Ask
and answer the questions.*

1. Was the briefcase big or little?
2. Was he short or tall?
3. Was he fat or thin?
4. What color was his jacket? his pants?
5. Describe the man's hair and face.

B. Verb Tense Review

In this book you learned to
use verbs in many forms.

PRESENT PROGRESSIVE:	**Are** you **going** to the club now?
SIMPLE PAST:	No, I **went** yesterday.
SIMPLE PRESENT:	But you **go** to the club every day.
INFINITIVE:	I know. But Dad told me **to study.**
FUTURE:	I'**m going to go** to the club tomorrow.

EXERCISE 7: *Detective Adams Finds the Suspect*

Complete the paragraph with the correct forms of the verbs in parentheses.

Mary Green **(1. feel)** _____ nervous every night, but tonight she isn't going to

worry. She **(2. be able)** _____ to sleep. Now Detective Adams **(3. tell)** _____

her about the suspect. The detective **(4. find)** _____ the man yesterday. How did the

detective find him? He **(5. describe)** _____ the suspect to Mary's neighbors. One neighbor

(6. know) _____ the suspect. The detective asked the neighbor **(7. drive)** _____

him to the man's house. Then Detective Adams **(8. take)** _____ the suspect to the police

station.

EXERCISE 8: *Questions and Answers*

Read each question. Write the letter of the answer on the line.
Watch the pronouns and verb tenses.

1. Were the chairs next to the table? _____
2. Is Alfonso's hair curly? _____
3. Is Maria going to sing? _____
4. Were you at the library? _____
5. Are they sleeping? _____
6. Is Ed handsome? _____
7. Was there anyone at the park? _____
8. Are you going to visit us? _____
9. Was the baby little? _____
10. Is there a police officer in the room? _____

a. No, she isn't.
b. Yes, they are.
c. No, they weren't.
d. Yes, he is.
e. Yes, there is.
f. No, it isn't.
g. Yes, she was.
h. Yes, we are.
i. No, I wasn't.
j. No, there wasn't.

LISTENING

Prelistening

A mystery story is a story about something that the writer does not explain until the end. Do you watch mystery programs on TV? Do you read mystery stories? Do you like mysteries? Why or why not?

EXERCISE 9: *What Do You Think Is Happening?*

*Listen to the mystery story. Answer the questions for each section after you hear it. Circle **T** for **true**. Circle **F** for **false**.*

A.
1. T F Two people are getting out of a car.
2. T F The people are nervous.

B.
1. T F Greg opened the door.
2. T F Carol and Greg are at the store.

C.
1. T F Sam and Paula live in the house.
2. T F Sam hears something.

D.
1. T F Greg is Sam's brother.
2. T F Sam's wife was afraid.

PRONUNCIATION

EXERCISE 10: *Words With S-Blends*

Listen to the words and repeat.

/st/	/sp/	/sl/	/sw/	/sk/	/sn/	/sm/	/str/
stand	Spain	sleeve	sweater	skirt	snack	small	strange
stone	Spanish	sleep	swim	school		smile	street
stop	speak	slept	swam				straight

EXERCISE 11: *Just for Fun*

Listen to the sentences. Then say them.

1. The six suspects stopped to eat snacks and sleep.
2. Mr. Smith swims at the school every Saturday.
3. Some strange spies are speaking Spanish to Miss Sloan.
4. Steve bought a sweater with short sleeves at the store.

EXERCISE 12: *Intonation of Questions*

A. *The intonation of **yes/no** questions usually rises. The intonation of information questions usually falls. Listen and repeat.*

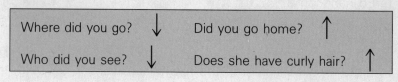

| Where did you go? ↓ | Did you go home? ↑ |
| Who did you see? ↓ | Does she have curly hair? ↑ |

B. *Listen to the questions. Is the intonation at the end of the question rising or falling? Circle the "down" arrow for falling intonation. Circle the "up" arrow for rising intonation.*

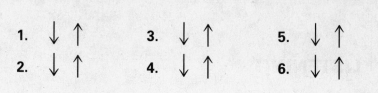

| 1. ↓ ↑ | 3. ↓ ↑ | 5. ↓ ↑ |
| 2. ↓ ↑ | 4. ↓ ↑ | 6. ↓ ↑ |

C. *Read the question. What kind of intonation do you think it has? Circle the correct arrow. Then say the question. Listen to the questions and check your answers.*

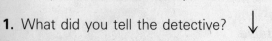 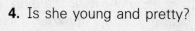 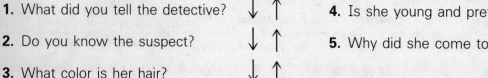 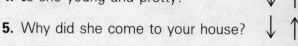

1. What did you tell the detective? ↓ ↑
2. Do you know the suspect? ↓ ↑
3. What color is her hair? ↓ ↑

4. Is she young and pretty? ↓ ↑
5. Why did she come to your house? ↓ ↑

SPEAKING

Work with a partner. Your partner wants you to meet a friend at the restaurant in the mall. You don't know the person. Ask your partner to describe the friend. Which person is it? Take turns.

Useful Language
Is your friend a male or a female?
Is (she) fat or thin?
Is (she) tall or short?
Does (she) have a big nose?

READING

Prereading

A good mystery writer makes the readers think that everyone is a suspect. One person in the picture below is a spy. He is going to put something in another person's drink. Who do you think is going to do it? Who do you think is going to drink it?

Who Did It?

There are four men in the room, two on the couch and one in each chair. Their last names are Smith, Brown, Robinson, and Osborn. One is a teacher, one is an actor, one is a pilot, and one is a doctor. There is a mirror across from the couch.

a. Mr. Smith's daughter takes a soft drink to Robinson, some tea to Osborn, and some coffee to Brown.
b. The actor looks in the mirror and sees the door close behind Smith's daughter.
c. Osborn is to the right of the actor.
d. The doctor is sitting in a chair on Brown's left.
e. Smith, Osborn, and Brown don't have sisters.
f. The doctor doesn't have anything to drink.
g. The pilot's brother-in-law is the actor. He's next to Osborn.
h. The pilot is sitting in a chair.
i. Robinson and the teacher put their cups on the same table.
j. Someone puts something in a cup of tea.

couch:

mirror: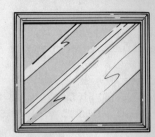

brother-in-law: the husband of your sister

cup:

EXERCISE 13: *Identifying the Suspects*

Work with a partner. You are detectives. Your job is to answer these questions. You will probably have to do Exercise 14 on page 100 before you can answer them.

1. Where are the people sitting? Write their names on the lines with **a.**
2. What are their occupations? Write their occupations on the lines with **b.**

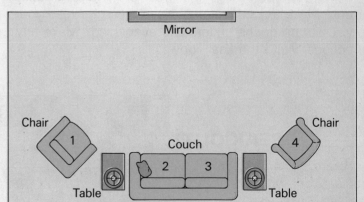

1. a. _____ **2. a.** _____ **3. a.** _____ **4. a.** _____
  b. _____   **b.** _____   **b.** _____   **b.** _____

EXERCISE 14: *More Clues*

Do you need more help to answer Exercise 13? Answer these questions. Then complete Exercise 13.

1. Look at clues A and F. Who is the doctor? _____

2. Look at clues E and G. Who is the pilot? _____

3. Look at clues D and H. Who are sitting on chairs? _____ _____

4. Look at clues C and G. Who is on the couch on the left? _____

   Who is on the couch on the right? _____

5. Look at clues B and G. Who is the actor? _____

6. Look at clues C and I. What is Osborn's occupation? _____

 WRITING

A. Prewriting. Writing. You are a mystery writer. Use these clues to write a story.

1. Time:

3.

5.

2.

4.

6.

B. Revising. Presenting. Read your story. Is everything correct? Make any corrections. Have a partner read your story. Does he or she understand everything? Make any corrections. Write the final copy.

 SPEAK OUT!

These are some famous people. Work with a partner. One partner thinks about one of the people. The other partner can ask five **yes/no** questions to try to guess who it is. Take turns.

Michael Jackson

Bill Cosby

Crystal Gayle

Paula Abdul

IRREGULAR VERBS

Base Form	Simple Past
be: am, is, are	was, were
build	built
buy	bought
come	came
do	did
drink	drank
drive	drove
eat	ate
find	found
fly	flew
get	got
go	went
have, has	had
hear	heard
know	knew
lose	lost
make	made
mean	meant
meet	met
put	put
read	read
ride	rode
run	ran
say	said
see	saw
sing	sang
sit	sat
sleep	slept
speak	spoke
stand	stood
swim	swam
take	took
tell	told
think	thought
understand	understood
wear	wore
win	won
write	wrote

THE INTERNATIONAL PHONETIC ALPHABET

IPA SYMBOLS

These symbols are used in In Contact.

/e/	**A**pril
/æ/	**a**pple
/ə/	**a**round
/ɔ/	**Au**gust
/b/	**b**ook
/k/	**c**at, **k**angaroo
/d/	**d**og
/i/	**ea**t
/ɛ/	**e**lephant
/f/	**f**ish
/g/	**g**irl
/h/	**h**ouse
/aɪ/	**i**ce
/ɪ/	**i**gloo
/ǰ/	**j**ar
/l/	**l**ion
/m/	**m**onkey
/n/	**n**urse
/ŋ/	si**ng**
/o/	**o**pen
/ɑ/	**o**ctopus
/aʊ/	h**ow**
/ɔɪ/	**oi**nk
/ʊ/	b**oo**k
/u/	sch**oo**l
/p/	**p**ig
/kw/	**qu**een
/r/	**r**abbit
/ɚ/	moth**er**
/ɝ/	**ear**th
/s/	**s**andwich
/š/	**sh**eep
/ž/	vi**s**ion
/t/	**t**able
/θ/	**th**ree
/ð/	**th**ese
/yu/	**u**niform
/ʌ/	**u**mbrella
/v/	**v**alentine
/w/	**w**ater
/ks/	bo**x**
/y/	**y**ellow
/z/	**z**ebra
/č/	**ch**air
/hw/	**wh**ale

THE ENGLISH ALPHABET

Here is the pronunciation of the letters of the English alphabet, written in International Phonetic Alphabet symbols.

a	/e/
b	/bi/
c	/si/
d	/di/
e	/i/
f	/ɛf/
g	/ǰi/
h	/eč/
i	/aɪ/
j	/ǰe/
k	/ke/
l	/ɛl/
m	/ɛm/
n	/ɛn/
o	/o/
p	/pi/
q	/kyu/
r	/ɑr/
s	/ɛs/
t	/ti/
u	/yu/
v	/vi/
w	/'dʌbəl,yu/
x	/ɛks/
y	/waɪ/
z	/zi/

Numbers indicate units in In Contact Book 1. *GS indicates Getting Started.*

a/an GS
about 3
across from 4
actor 1
actress 1
ad 7
address 2
adult 10
afraid 8
afternoon GS
to agree 10
airport 2
All right. 10
alone 8
and 1
angry 8
to answer 1
any 4
anyone 12
apple 7
April 5
around 11
article 10
to ask 1
at 2
August 5

baby 10
backpack GS
banana 7
basketball 7
to be (am/is/are)
  1
to be (was/were)
  8
to be able (to do
  something) 11
to be born 9
beautiful 9
because 8
behind 6
to believe 11
between 4
big 10

bike 3
birthday 5
black 4
blackboard GS
blond 12
blue 4
book GS
box 12
boy 2
bread 5
breakfast 7
briefcase GS
brother 3
brown 4
to build/built 9
building 9
bus GS
business 2
but 3
butter 5
to buy/bought 4
bye GS

cake 5
calendar 9
to call 8
camera 6
can/can't 3
Can you help me?
  GS
car GS
to carry 6
chair 12
chalk GS
cheese 5
chocolate 5
city 2
class GS
clean 10
clear 11
clerk 2
to climb 9
clock 6
to close GS

clothes 4
cloudy 11
club 7
clue 12
coffee 5
cold 11
color 4
to come/came 4
confused 8
to cook 3
to cry 8
curly 12

to dance 3
date 9
daughter 3
day 4
December 5
dentist 1
to describe 12
to design 4
desk GS
detective 12
different (from)
  11
dinner 7
dirty 10
to disagree 10
to discover 9
to do/did 3
doctor 1
door GS
down 11
dress 4
to drink/drank 5
to drive/drove 3
driver 1
drum 2

ear 12
early 10
Earth 11
easy 7
to eat/ate 3

egg 5
eight 1
eighteen 2
eighty 3
eleven 1
eraser GS
evening GS
every 5
everyone 12
Excuse me. 2
exercise 7
to explain 3
eye 12

face 12
false 3
family 3
famous 9
fat 10
father 3
favorite 8
February 5
feeling 8
female 12
fifteen 1
fifty 3
to fill in 2
to find/found 9
to find out/found
  out 10
fine GS
first 2
five 1
to fly/flew 3
to follow 6
food 5
foot/feet 12
for 4
form 2
forty 3
four 1
fourteen 1
free *(no cost)* 10
Friday 4

friend 2
from 1
fruit 7
fun 7
future 11

to get/got 6
to get/got married
  11
to get/got off 6
to get/got on 6
girl 2
glasses 6
to go/went GS
good GS
good-by GS
good night GS
granddaughter 3
grandfather 3
grandmother 3
grandson 3
grape 7
great 5
green 4
to guess 11
guitar 2

hair 12
hamburger 5
hand GS
handsome 12
to happen 6
happy 8
hard 7
to have, has/had
  2
Have a nice
  (vacation). 2
he 1
healthy 7
to hear/heard 12
hello GS
her 1
here 10

Here it is./Here
   they are. 2
hi GS
him 8
his 1
history 9
home 8
homework 8
horoscope 11
hospital 2
hot 11
hot dog 5
hotel 2
hour 8
house 8
How (strange)! 6
How about (this
   shirt)? 4
How are you?
   GS
How do you feel?
   8
How long? 8
How often? 7
hungry 5
husband 3

I 1
I can't stand it! 8
idea 5
I'd like (some
   cake). 5
important 3
I'm sorry. GS
in 2
inch 12
information 10
in front of 6
in love 8
in shape 7
interesting 3
interview 10
to introduce 1
it 1
I think/don't think
   so. 12
its 5

jacket 4
January 5
jeans 4
job 10
juice 7
July 5
to jump (rope) 7
June 5
to know/knew
   GS
to know how/
   knew how 7

large 4
last 2
late 10
to laugh 8
to learn 9
Let's (go). 5
letter 6
lettuce 5
to lift (weights) 7
light 12
to like 4
to listen GS
little 12
to live 2
long 4
to look at GS
to look for 9
to lose/lost 9
a lot of 7
to love 8
lunch 7

magazine 6
mail carrier 6
to make/made 3
to make/made a
   mistake 10
male 12
mall 4
man/men 2
March 5
May 5
May I have (your
   form)? 2
me 8
Me, neither. 7
Me, too. 7
meal 7
to mean/meant 2
to meet/met 1
member 7
milk 5
minute 8
missing 12
Monday 4
money 6
month 5
moon 9
more 10
morning GS
mother 3
motorcycle 6
mountain 9
mouth 12
Mr. GS
Mrs. GS
Ms. GS
musician 2
my 1

name 1
to need 5
neighbor 6
nervous 8
new 6
news (the) 10
newspaper 6
next to 4
nice 1
Nice to meet you.
   1
night GS
nine 1
nineteen 2
ninety 3
no 1
no one 12
nose 12
November 5
now 6
number 1
nurse 1

occupation 1
o'clock 6
October 5
of 5
of course GS
office 2
OK GS
old 5
on 2
one 1
one hundred 3
one thousand 3
onion 5
on sale 4
to open GS
opinion 10
or 3
orange (adj.) 4
orange (noun) 7
our 5
out of shape 7
over 11

pants 4
paper GS
park 6
past 11
pen GS
pencil GS
people 2
person 6
phone 10
piano 2
picture GS
pie 3
piece 5
pilot 1

pink 4
pizza 5
place 2
plane GS
plant 3
to play 2
please GS
police/police
   officer 12
pool 7
post card 9
to predict 11
pretty 10
problem 5
purple 4
to put/put 12

question 1

radio 10
rainy, to rain 11
to raise GS
to read/read 3
ready 1
real 9
red 4
to remember 9
to repeat GS
to report 10
to return 6
to ride/rode 3
right 1
ring 8
room 7
ruins 9
to run/ran 3

sad 8
salad 5
salesperson 4
the same (as) 11
sandwich 5
Saturday 4
to say/said 8
school 2
scientist 11
second 9
secretary 1
to see/saw 7
See you later. 7
September 5
seven 1
seventeen 2
seventy 3
she 1
shirt 4
shocked 8
shoe 4
to shop 4
short 4

sick 8
to sing/sang 3
sister 3
to sit/sat (down)
   GS
six 1
sixteen 2
sixty 3
skirt 4
to sleep/slept 12
sleeve 4
small 4
to smile 8
snack 7
snowy, to snow
   11
soap opera 8
sock 4
soft drink 5
some 4
someone 12
son 3
soon 11
space 11
to speak/spoke 2
to spell 1
spy 6
to stand/stood (up)
   GS
star 9
stone 9
to stop 6
store 4
story 6
straight 12
strange 6
street 2
student 1
sugar 5
suitcase 2
sun 9
Sunday 4
sunny 11
suspect 12
sweater 4
to swim/swam 3

T-shirt 4
table 12
to take/took 9
to take/took a
   picture 6
to talk 3
tall 10
taxi 1
tea 5
teacher 1
telephone 10
telescope 11
to tell/told 10

ten 1
terrible 8
test 9
thanks GS
thank you GS
that 3
That's amazing!
  11
theater 2
their 5
them 8
there 4
these 4
they 1
thin 10
thing GS
to think/thought
  6
third 9
thirsty 5
thirteen 1
thirty 3
this GS
those 4
thousand 3
three 1
Thursday 4
ticket 2
tired GS
to GS
today 5
tomato 5
tomorrow 11
tonight 7
too 2
true 3
Tuesday 4
to turn off/on 12
TV 7
twelve 1
twenty 2
two 1
to type 3

ugly 10
under 11
to understand/
  understood GS
up 11
us 8

vacation 2
very GS

to wait (for) 6
to walk 3

to want 4
war 9
watch 6
to watch 7
water 7
we 1
to wear/wore 4
weather 11
Wednesday 4
week 4
weekend 10
well GS
What? GS
What do you do?
  1
What does he/she
  do? 1
What kind? 7
What's the
  weather like?
  11
What time is it?
  6
When? 5
Where? 1
Which? 6
white 4
Who? 6
Why? 8
Why don't you
  (start)? 9
wife/wives 3
to win/won 9
window GS
windy 11
with 4
without 4
woman/women 2
word 1
to work 2
worried 8
Would you like...?
  10
to write/wrote 3
wrong 1

year 5
yellow 4
yes 1
yesterday 8
you 1
young 12
your 1
You're welcome.
  2

INDEX

Numbers indicate units in Book 1. GS indicates Getting Started.